The Earth Needed You

WRITTEN BY
Melissa Mangiapanella

ILLUSTRATED BY
Bilal Ihsan

Copyright © 2021 Melissa Mangiapanella

All rights reserved. No part of this publication may be reproduced, distributed, or transmitted in any form or by any means, including photocopying, recording, or other electronic or mechanical methods, without prior written permission of the publisher, except in the case of brief quotations embodied in critical reviews and certain other noncommercial uses permitted by copyright law. For permission requests, write to the author at the email address below.

ISBN: 978-1-68564-114-6

Library of Congress Control Number: 2022900185

Images by Bilal Ihsan.

Book design by Travis D. Peterson of Launch Mission Creative

Printed by IngramSpark
First printing edition 2022

Melissa Mangiapanella
Sarasota, Florida
MelissaDMangiapanella@gmail.com

For my Greyson Andrew.

The Earth needed you.

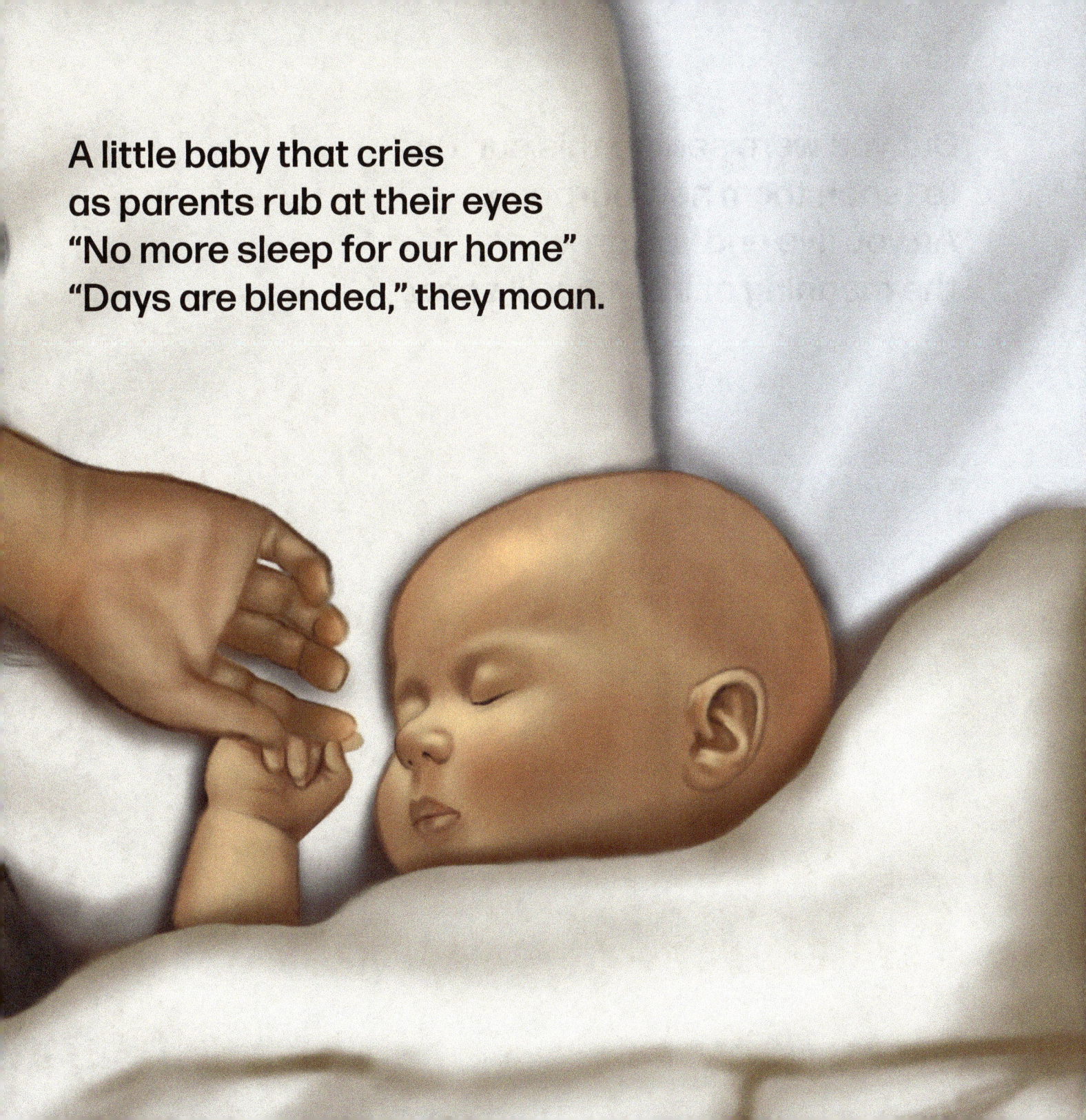

A little baby that cries
as parents rub at their eyes
"No more sleep for our home"
"Days are blended," they moan.

But you were sent to this surface
to teach them new purpose.
As you live and you grow
the meaning of life you will show.

*Because the
Earth needed you.*

Little friends you will meet
snuggle with socks on their feet
in houses a row.
Good nights are in tow.

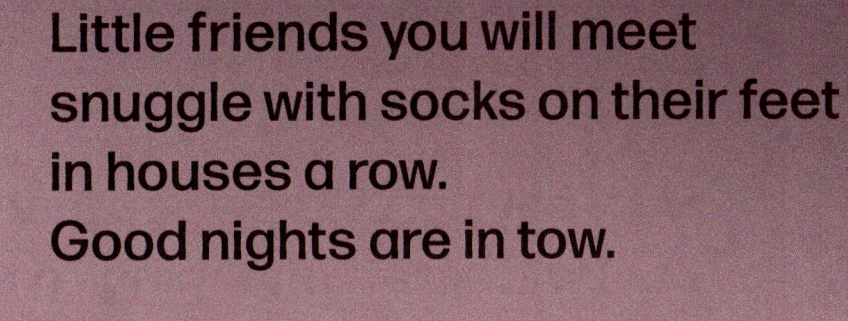

They don't know you just yet,
but there's one thing I'd bet.
You will help shape their lives
with every high and low five.

*The Earth
needed you.*

Your teachers may not smile
as they proof read with red ink
at the silly way you dot your "i"
or when you speak before you think.

But your imagination will remind them
when the papers stack up tall,
of why they were called to be the ones
to work harder than them all.

The Earth needed you.

And then one day you'll find your passion,
it may fly in like a plane
or slowly slip into your days,
like sunlight through a window pane.

But the beauty that's inside you
please share for all to see
because you're the only one who can
change the world the way it needs to be.

The Earth needed you.

He or she is waiting for you.

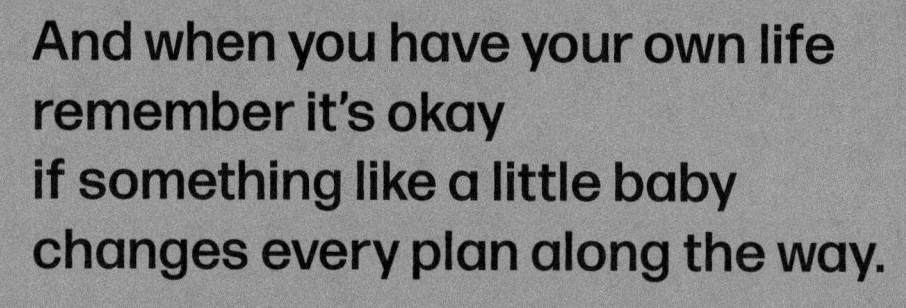

And when you have your own life
remember it's okay
if something like a little baby
changes every plan along the way.

Because babies are sent to this surface
to teach our great big hearts new purpose.
As they live and learn and love and grow
because of you we now know,
the meaning of life they will show.

Melissa Mangiapanella is a poet, writer and author of the new children's book *The Earth Needed You*. As a professionally trained writer and educator, Melissa has a MFA in English and a MFA in Special Education from Molloy College, as well as a BFA in Journalism from Adelphi University. Melissa is the author of the popular book, *Pea-ple of the World*, which illustrates diverse family structures spoken through forms of various peas in pods. The messages she writes are always for the children that still need to hear these words, adults looking to express what they cannot and a reiteration for her own children if they need or a lesson that not everyone is growing up just like them if they don't. She believes strongly in healing through art.

You can reach Melissa at
melissadmangiapanella@gmail.com

Illustrated by Bilal Ihsan
info@letsillustrate.org

www.ingramcontent.com/pod-product-compliance
Lightning Source LLC
LaVergne TN
LVHW060054080526
838200LV00085B/208